To Phil Straw

with special thanks for your unflagging support and friendship from beginning to end

Thank you to the many friends who have helped,

especially Miren, Haydn, and David

First U.S. edition 2016

Library of Congress Catalog Card Number 2014960102
ISBN 978-0-7636-7966-8

16 17 18 19 20 21 CCP 10 9 8 7 6 5 4 3 2 1

Printed in Shenzhen, Guangdong, China

This book was typeset in Humana Sans.
The artwork was prepared as collage constructions,
which were reproduced in full color from photographs by Jaime Plaza.

Image of globe on page 45 reproduced courtesy of Mountain High Maps©
Copyright © 1993 Digital Wisdom©, Inc.

Candlewick Press
99 Dover Street
Somerville, Massachusetts 02144

visit us at www.candlewick.com

JEANNIE BAKER

Circle

In its lifetime a godwit will usually fly farther

than the distance from the earth to the moon.

CANDLEWICK PRESS

In a place where mud and sand become sea . . .

a godwit with white wing patches
flies up with his flock.

The moment is right
for the long journey north.

The flock flies high
above the clouds,
chattering at times
to help stay close together.
Each bird takes a turn
to lead the way.

They follow an ancient,
invisible pathway
for six nights
and six days,
until they know they need to stop.

The flock floats down beneath the clouds,
each bird looking for food and somewhere safe to rest.
But the places they remember are gone.

They search in wider and wider circles.

Eventually the godwits find a safe stretch of mud.

At low tide the mud teems with food.
The godwit with white patches
eats day and night.

Days turn to weeks and still he eats,
until his body is swollen with fat
and it's time to move on . . .

on with another flock . . .

on and on . . .

following the ancient, invisible pathway
until they reach their northern home.

Now the godwit with white patches flies on alone,
back to his remembered place.

He scrapes a shallow nest
in the ground.

Awika-wika-wika-wikraaaaaaaaaa-wika-wika-wik . . .

His singing rings across the land.
Dancing wildly through the air
in steep, twisting, graceful dives,
finally, he attracts a mate.

Soon the godwits guard
four perfect eggs, and then four
newly hatched chicks,
taking turns to keep them warm.

A hungry fox finds the nest
and won't be stopped.

One chick hides,
crouched and still,
disappearing into
the colors of the land.

Weeks pass.
The chick is almost full-grown,
and the godwits know it's time to move on.

The mother godwit leaves first.

The godwit with white patches goes next.

Their grown chick will follow later.

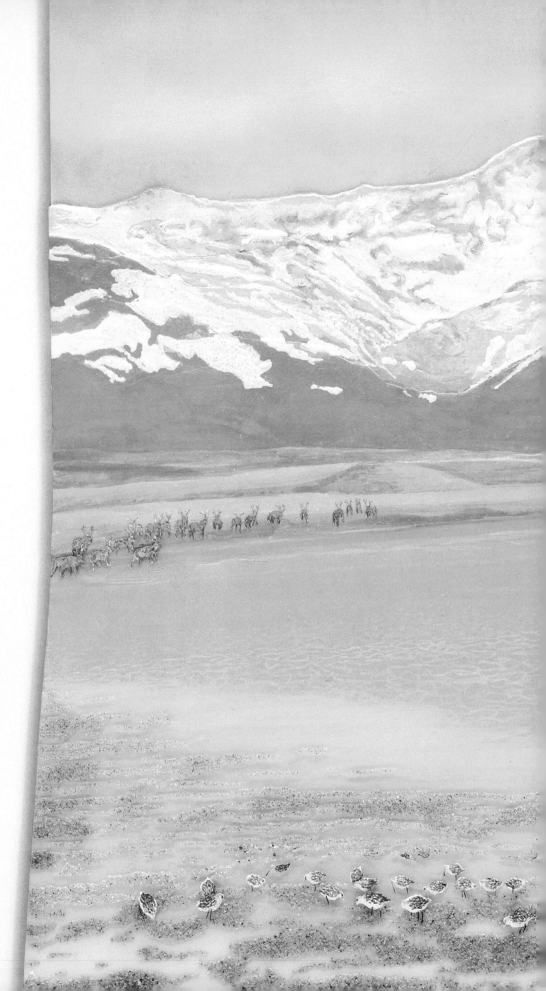

The godwits join other birds
at a feeding place on the shore.

The godwit with white patches
grows white and gray-brown feathers.
He becomes strong and fat.

But the days grow colder,
and finding food is harder.

Late one afternoon,
when the wind is icy,
godwits call to each other.

The time is right.
Suddenly they leave as one.

Following an ancient, invisible pathway
high above the clouds,
each bird takes a turn to lead the way south.

Alone in an infinity of sky, the tiny birds fly
on and on and on for nine nights and nine days,
without stopping . . .

until they reach the other side of the world.

The flock drops down beneath the clouds,
each bird searching for a safe place to settle.

The godwit with white wing patches
rests at last . . .

back in the place where mud and sand become sea.

NATURE RESERVE
Dogs, horses, vehicles prohibited

Author's Note

The bar-tailed godwits (Limosa lapponica baueri) in this story make the longest unbroken journey of any animal in the world. Before each Arctic winter they migrate more than 7,000 miles (11,265 kilometers) from their northern home in Alaska to their southern home in Australia and New Zealand, without even stopping to rest.

On their return to the north, the godwits need to stop and feed in the wetlands of Asia, especially those around the Yellow Sea. Wetlands are important for migrating waterbirds as they provide areas where the birds can rest and find food, enabling them to complete their journeys. The Yellow Sea wetlands are rapidly disappearing as a result of land reclamation and development, and the godwits and other migrating shorebirds are finding it harder and harder to find places where they can rest and feed.

The annual movements across the world of millions of birds, sea creatures, and other animals remind us that everything in nature is interdependent and connected. The changes we make on one side of the world can have consequences on another. The challenge we face now is how to live without destroying the places that are crucial to shorebirds' age-old, wondrous circle of life.

For more information on godwits and shorebirds:
www.globalflywaynetwork.com.au
www.awsg.org.au
www.miranda-shorebird.org.nz

Godwits' Migration Map

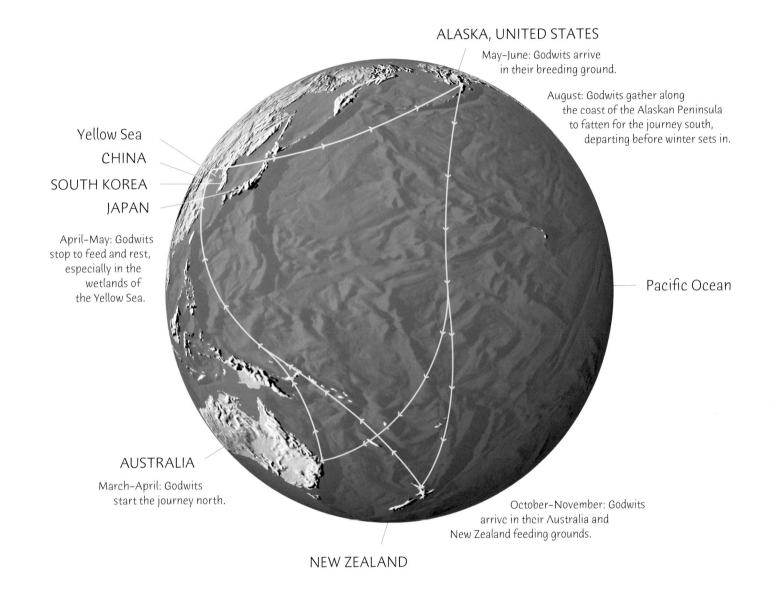

ALASKA, UNITED STATES

May–June: Godwits arrive
in their breeding ground.

August: Godwits gather along
the coast of the Alaskan Peninsula
to fatten for the journey south,
departing before winter sets in.

Yellow Sea

CHINA

SOUTH KOREA

JAPAN

April–May: Godwits
stop to feed and rest,
especially in the
wetlands of
the Yellow Sea.

Pacific Ocean

AUSTRALIA

March–April: Godwits
start the journey north.

October–November: Godwits
arrive in their Australia and
New Zealand feeding grounds.

NEW ZEALAND

Other migrating creatures in this book

Green turtles
Great knots
Arctic tern
Sandhill cranes
Brent geese
Caribou

Short-tailed albatross
Humpback whales
Curlew
Channel-billed cuckoo
Black-winged stilts